**Words © South Hand Music, ASCAP
All Illustrations © Darren Thompson 1998
Design and Layout by Jennifer Cole
ISBN 0-9661407-1-0**

"I never had a piece of Toast
Particularly long and wide
But fell upon the sanded floor,
And always on the buttered side."

—James Payne 1884

I don't want to brag,
I don't want to boast.
I just tell'em
I like Toast

I get up in the morning about 6 A.M.

Have a little jelly,
Have a little jam

**Take a piece of bread, put it in the slot
Push down the lever and the wires get hot.**

I get toast!

Now there's no secret to toasting perfection

There's a dial on the side
And you make your selection

**Push to the Dark or the light, and then,
If it pops too soon, press down again.**

And make Toast,

When the first cavemen drove in from the dregs,

He didn't know
What would go
With the bacon
and the eggs.

Must have been a genius,
Got it in his head
Plugged the toaster in the wall
and bought a loaf of bread.

And made Toast,

Oh, oui, oui, Monsieur Bon jour croquette,

Uh huh Croissant, Chevy Corvette.

Maurice Chevalier, Eiffel Tower
Oh, oui Marie, Baguette Bon Soir

So, , In Chicago

Or on the North Pole